The question that won't go away:

WHY DOESN'T GOD *DO* SOMETHING?

A BOLD AND HONEST LOOK AT THE ETERNAL QUESTION

Ronald Higdon

Energion Publications
Gonzalez, FL
2017

Electronic ISBNs:
Adobe Digital Editions: 978-1-63199-484-5
iBooks: 978-1-63199-485-2
Kindle: 978-1-63199-486-9
Google Play: 978-1-63199-487-6

ISBN13: 978-1-63199-479-1
LCCN: 2017962267

Energion Publications
P.O. Box 841
Gonzalez, FL 32560

energion.com
pubs@energion.com

DEDICATION

Through the course of over fifty-five years of pastoral ministry, many have come to me with aching hearts and burning questions. It had nothing to do with abandoning their faith, but everything to do with finding a place in that faith for the kinds of questions that would not go away. And, often, the kinds of questions they dared not ask in an open discussion.

Through these conversations, I have come to a greater understanding of what it means to feel that God simply wasn't living up to the reputation given them by sincere Sunday School teachers and people of confident faith. In response to their prayers, they received no response. While believing that "nothing is impossible with God," they saw no action to verify such a maxim.

This book is dedicated to all who have ever cried out "Why?" in the face of inexplicable tragedy and loss. It is dedicated to all of those who want to know that it is okay to bring honest questions and shaking heads to God in prayer. It is dedicated to all of those who need to discover that they are in the company of a great cloud of witnesses, both in Holy Scripture and the community of God's people down through the ages. I want them to be assured they can count me among their number.

TABLE OF CONTENTS

PREFACE

In the space of one week I was labeled "unthinking" and "unbiblical." This was not in a public forum but came about as the result of reading two different publications. The first was a national religious magazine in which a writer in a letter to the editor stated that "thinking Christians" couldn't possibly come to any other conclusion. The second was from an author who wrote that "biblical believers" all come to a particular point of view. What both writers actually asserted was that their interpretation was the only correct one. Here is an excerpt from the book mentioned above:

> *What is different about this book? First, this work attempts to be clear about the various dilemmas and the proposed solutions.... Second, this book is concise.... Third, this book is comprehensive.... Fourth, this book attempts to be correct. We are not engaging in mere intellectual exercises; we are searching for the truth.*[1]

Now in my eighth decade of life, I have grown increasingly wary (and weary) of those who believe that if others do not agree with their perspective or interpretation, their ideas and opinions can be written off as invalid, incorrect, and not worthy of a hearing. Genuine and healthy dialogue comes when respectful listening is the ground rule. At one time, my denomination prided itself on "the right to fellowship across honest differences of opinion." Then documents began to be issued which stated the "official" and "sanctioned" beliefs necessary to keep one in good standing. Many of us found ourselves listed as the "unqualified." The tragedy is that those who issued the documents *sincerely* believed that the points of view expressed were the only legitimate ones.

The tragedy of such actions, in both the religious and political realms, violates freedom of expression and freedom of conscience.

---

1   Geisler, Normal L., *If God, Why Evil?* (Minneapolis: Bethany House, 2011), 10.

People are no longer able to publicly express their fears, doubts, and honest questions. In so many areas, life is far too complex for "final" answers given by "experts." As we deal with the mysteries, paradoxes, and ambiguities of life we need the myriad of voices that forces us to focus on the easily overlooked dark corners. Although it is my purpose in this book to be biblically and intellectually honest, I do not claim infallibility. I simply invite you to explore with me as I grapple with the question that has never been "settled."

This is a book intended for personal reflection and group discussion. This means that personally you must be unafraid to look deeply into your own soul and listen to everything you hear there, even those things you would be most hesitant to tell others. Healthy group discussions provide a safe place for the sharing of all ideas – even those that make some in the group feel threatened (for whatever reasons). Respectful listening does not mean you must abandon your convictions or deeply held beliefs; it means you recognize that someone else's convictions and deeply held beliefs that differ from yours deserve a legitimate place in the discussion.

The question that won't go away that forms the basis for this book is summarized in these lines:

> *The fact of evil constitutes the most serious objection there is to the Christian belief in a God of love. The problem dealt with in this book is thus a theological one: Can the presence of evil in the world be reconciled with the existence of a God who is unlimited both in goodness and in power? If God is perfectly good, He must want to abolish all evil: but evil exists; therefore, God is not perfectly good or He is not infinitely powerful.*[2]

I promise you a bold and honest look at the question that won't go away. My purpose and request are identical with those made by Peter Kreeft in his book *Making Sense Out of Suffering:*

---

2   Hick, John, *Evil and the God of Love* (New York: Harper & Row, 1977), vii, 3, 5.

This book is not a neat set of answers for believers to beat unbelievers with. It is a record of a real, honest, personal quest, a lived journey of exploration in life's darkest cave. I do not ask or expect everyone to agree with me at the beginning of the journey, or at the end, only to come along.[3]

---

3   Kreeft, Peter, *Making Sense Out of Suffering* (Ann Arbor: Servant Books, 1986), 17.

THE CONTINUING QUESTION FROM LIFE

"O God, save me! God deliver me. Let me be free! Is there any God? Why am I a slave?" Frederick Douglass from his autobiography about his life as a slave, Narrative of the Life of Frederick Douglass, written in 1845.[4]

Life is good, and there's no reason to think it won't be – right up until the moment when everything explodes into a fireball of tiny, unrecognizable fragments, or it all goes skidding sideways, through the guardrail, over the embankment, and down the mountain. This will happen - and probably more than once.[5]

It was my first church out of seminary and the challenges were many because I was expected to be a pastor "in the know." As I stood by the bedside of his seven-year-old daughter who was dying from leukemia, I will never forget the grief and despair that darkened the father's conversation with me. "Pastor, I just don't understand. So many people have prayed for my little girl – the entire church has supported me with their thoughts and prayers for her recovery. The Bible tells us that God answers prayer, and that when his faithful people pray, healing and even miracles can be expected. Why didn't God do something for my daughter?"

I felt that a wiser, more experienced minister, would have been able to offer a good answer to his question but I had none. All I could do was stand with him in his grief and impending loss.

---

4   Douglass, Frederick, *Narrative of the Life of Frederick Douglass* (New York: Fall River Press, 2012), 61.

5   Fox, Michael J., *A Funny Thing Happened on the Way to the Future* (New York: Hyperion, 2010), 82.

Now in my eighties, you might suppose that a larger measure of theological wisdom would be mine. I regret to report that I still have no answer for that father's question which has come to me repeatedly during my half-century-plus of pastoral ministry. I also regret to report that after reading literally hundreds of books, attending countless workshops, and having extended conversations with ministerial colleagues in many parts of the country, I have found no one who has been able to supply a satisfactory answer to the question.

What I have discovered instead is a plethora of new questions that greatly expand the dimensions of the initial question. These new questions for me begin in the very first book of the Bible. Genesis hardly gets underway until the reader is confronted with unbelievable inaction on the part of the Creator. If you have missed it, permit me to give you a candid reading from the fourth chapter.

Both Cain and Abel bring offerings to the Lord even though at this point in Scripture there has been no command for any kind of an offering. For reasons we are not told, the Lord has no regard for Cain's offering, while Abel's offering is favorably received. God appears to be taken aback by the sibling rivalry that rears its ugly head and asks Cain, *"Why are you angry? Why has your countenance fallen? If you do well, will you not be accepted?"* (Genesis 4:7).

Most modern commentators agree that the issue does not involve what the brothers bring as an offering. Abel is a shepherd so he naturally brings a lamb; Cain is a farmer so he naturally brings a grain offering. "Doing well" evidently must have to do with Cain's attitude which is evident in the anger after his offering doesn't make the cut. The Lord speaks directly to a major problem when he warns Cain, *"If you do not do well, sin is lurking at the door; its desire is for you, but you must master it."*

The next time God shows up is after sin's attack is successful and Abel's blood cries out to God from the ground. My question: if God knows how dangerous the situation is, why doesn't he stick around to protect Abel? Why does he go off somewhere else while Cain invites his brother out to the field? Many sermons have been preached on God's question to Cain, *"Where is your brother Abel?"* (Genesis 4:9). God knows where he is and simply arrives too late on the scene to give this story a happy ending. For those who believe everything will turn out okay, the biblical story doesn't get very far until it proclaims, "Not necessarily!"

However, you read this text, the shocking conclusion is: God stands by and permits a good innocent man to be killed by a brother who refuses to keep his anger in check. But that is not the end of the shocks. The Hebrew Scriptures contain many verses about an eye for an eye and the forfeiture of life for the taking of a life. Capital punishment was the rule of the day. But instead of condemning Cain, as one would expect, God places a mark on him to protect him from anyone who might be tempted to administer justice on behalf of Cain.

Why didn't God do something for Abel?

The examples I have mentioned are special. But the strongest case against God comes not from them but from the billions of normal lives that are full of apparently pointless suffering. It is not that the suffering is not deserved; it is that it seems random and pointless, distributed according to no rhyme or reason but mere chance, and working no good, no end. For everyone who becomes a hero and a saint through suffering, there are ten who seem to become dehumanized, depressed, or despairing.[6]

What I promise you in the following pages is honesty, openness, and clarity from one in his eighties who continues the journey seeking to keep eyes and mind and heart attentive to fresh winds of the Spirit and the pursuit of a faith that stands the test of the assaults and tragedies of life that defy simplistic explanations. I believe you will find this to be a worthwhile journey.

Each of the ten brief chapters can be read easily in one sitting. The questions at the end are for your personal reflection and for discussion if the book is used in a study. Most of the 25 strategies in the conclusion are perspectives that I have found necessary in

---

6   Kreeft, Peter, *Making Sense Out of Suffering*, 10.

order to make some sense of the onslaught of the labeled evils in life that just keep coming.

Your suggestions and feedback are welcomed and can be sent to <u>rbooks5000@aol.com</u>.

THE CONTINUING QUESTION FROM THE BIBLE'S PRAYER BOOK

If you are selective in your reading of Scripture you will have no problem coming up with a positive and thoroughly hopeful stance on the question of God's involvement in our lives. But when refusing to hopscotch, you must take into account the cries of those who wonder where God is and just why he is not living up to his commitments.

The most obvious place to begin our search for these laments is in the book of Psalms, the prayer book and hymn book of Israel (Jesus' prayer book and hymnal). Psalm 77 poses six questions many never expect to find in what they know as "the praise book of the Bible":

1. Will the Lord reject forever?
2. Will he never show his favor again?
3. Has his unfailing love vanished forever?
4. Has his promise failed for all time?
5. Has God forgotten to be merciful?
6. Has he in anger withheld his compassion?

As many as fifty percent of the one-hundred-fifty psalms have been labeled "psalms of lament." Here are some of the verses we find in those psalms:

GOD SEEMS TO BE SLEEPING:

> *Arise, O Lord, in anger!*
> *Stand up against the fury of my enemies!*
> *Wake up, my God, and bring justice. (7:6).*

> *Then the Lord rose up*
> *as though waking from sleep…. (78:65).*

PERHAPS GOD IS DEAF:

> *I cry to you, Yahweh, my Rock! Do not be*
> *deaf to me, for if you are silent, I shall go down*
> *to the Pit like the rest. (28:1 - JB).*

IF GOD DOES HEAR, HE REMAINS SILENT:

> *Let our God come,*
> *and be silent no more! (50:3 – JB).*

> *God, do not remain silent…. (83:1a –JB).*

GOD IS AWAY SOMEWHERE IN HIDING:

> *O Lord, why do you stand so far away?*
> *Why do you hide*
> *when I need you the most? (10:1).*

> *How much longer will you forget me, Yah-*
> *weh? Forever? How much longer will you hide*
> *your face from me? How much longer must I*
> *endure grief in my soul, and sorry in my heart by*
> *day and night? (13:1-2 – JB).*

> *O Lord, do not stay away! (22:19a).*

> *Your favor, Yahweh, stood me on a peak*
> *impregnable; but then you hid your face and I*
> *was terrified. (30:7 – JB).*

> *God, hear my prayer, do not hide from my*
> *petition, give me a hearing, answer me, I cannot*
> *rest for complaining. (55:1 – JB).*

WE ARE EXPERIENCING FEELINGS OF REJECTION AND ABANDONMENT:

> *God, we have heard with our own ears,*
> *our ancestors have told us of the deeds you per-*
> *formed in their days, in days long ago by your*
> *hand. Yet now you abandon and scorn us, you*
> *no longer march with our armies, you allow the*
> *enemy to push us back, and let those who hate*
> *us raid us when it suits them. (44:1, 9 – JB).*

> *O God, why have you rejected us forever?*
> *Why is your anger so intense against the sheep*
> *of your own pasture? (74:1).*

GOD IS NOT DOING ANYTHING:

> *Yahweh, how long will you be? Come back,*
> *Yahweh, rescue my soul, save me,*
> *if you love me. (6:3b-4 – JB).*

> *How long, O Lord, will you look on*
> *and do nothing? (35:17a).*

> *O God, don't sit idly by,*
> *silent and inactive! (83:1).*

THE WICKED CONTINUE TO PROSPER:

> *Look at them: these are the wicked,*
> *well-off and still getting richer!   (73:12 - JB).*

> *How much longer, God, is the oppressor to*
> *blaspheme, is the enemy to insult your name*
> *forever? Why hold back your hand, why keep*
> *your right hand hidden? (74:10 – JB).*

> *Yahweh, how much longer are the wicked,*
> *how much longer are the wicked*
> *to triumph? (94:3 – JB).*

> *O God, if only you would destroy*
> *the wicked! (139:19a).*

BEING GOOD HASN'T PAID OFF

> *All this has happened despite*
> *our loyalty to you. (44:17),*

> *All this happened to us though we had not*
> *forgotten you, though we had not been disloyal*
> *to your covenant.... (44:17 – JB).*

> *Was it for nothing that I kept my heart pure*
> *and kept myself from doing wrong? All I get is*
> *trouble all day long; every morning brings me*
> *pain. (73:13-14).*

GOD'S ACHIEVEMENTS SEEM TO BE ALL PAST-TENSE:

> *"This," I said then, "is what distresses me:*
> *that the power of the Most High is no longer*
> *what it was." (77:11 – JB).*

In keeping with the spirit of many of the psalms, the late John Claypool wrote a moving account of the death of his daughter. Many were upset by his honesty and couldn't believe a minister would write anything except about the triumph of his faith in such a situation. But his questions are the same questions asked in many of the psalms. They are also our questions.

> *I do not believe God wants me to hold in these questions that burn in my heart and soul —question like "Why is there leukemia? Why are children of promise cut down at the age of ten? Why did you let Laura Lue suffer so excruciatingly and then let her die?" I am really honoring God when I come clean and say, "You owe me an explanation."*[7]

Making the Psalms your prayer book will enable you to stay in touch with the ups and downs of life and faith. The prayers will help you to see the many emotions that fill those prayers, the questions that abound, and the fluctuations that have always been a part of the life of God's people. These psalms were not written by agnostics or atheists. No writer ever expressed doubt about God's existence; the complaint was about his inaction.

QUESTIONS FOR REFLECTION AND DISCUSSION

1. Are you surprised that this frequently labeled "praise book" contains so many complaints?
2. Which of the listed references from the Psalms produced the most emotional response? Why do you think this was so?
3. What are some of the "explanations" you have heard that attempted to tone down the rhetoric of the psalmists?
4. What lessons have you taken from these references about your personal prayer life?
5. Since the book of Psalms was the worship book for ancient Israel, what kind of worship do you think was experienced when the psalms of lament were used?

---

7   Claypool, John, *Tracks of a Fellow Struggler* (Waco: Word Books, 1974), 75.

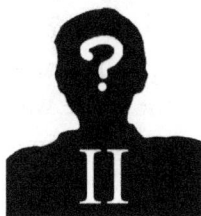

II DOES JOB PROVIDE ANY LIGHT ON THE SUBJECT?

Philip Yancy writes:

> *Job has put God on trial, accusing him of unfair acts against an innocent party.... But chapters 1 and 2 prove that, regardless of what Job thinks, God is not on trial in this book. Job is on trial. The point of the book is not suffering: Where is God when it hurts? The prologue dealt with that issue. The point is faith: Where is Job when it hurts? How is he responding? To understand the book of Job, I must begin there.*[8]

For many years all I knew about the book of Job was that it dealt with the problem of suffering. Of course, it doesn't. It deals with a much bigger problem. Instead of answering the question, "Why do good people suffer so many bad things?" it raises a number of other questions: Is life some kind of game between the powers of good and the powers of evil? How could a good God allow someone as faithful as Job to be the subject of a contest in which he loses almost everything dear to him? How could God sit idly by for thirty-seven of forty-two chapters while Job's friends accuse him of protesting too much about a fate he certainly must deserve? When God finally shows up how could he possibly be so lacking in compassion and mercy that when he *answers* Job (a word directly from Job 38:1) he does so by pummeling him with questions? And doesn't it seem grossly unfair that Job is never made aware of the heavenly council contest that brought about all his suffering?

---

8 Yancey, Phillip, *Disappointment With God* (Grand Rapids: Zondervan Publishing House, 1988), 165.

Job is one of the "wisdom" books of the Hebrew Scriptures and I believe it has much to offer us but its wisdom is not a solution to the ongoing problem of theodicy. I always begin any study of the book of Job by pointing out that the first two chapters and most of the last chapter are written in prose; the remaining thirty-nine chapters are poetry. For those who read this book the same way they read the books of Samuel, Kings, and Chronicles, hardly anything makes sense. A beginning place for understanding Scripture is to know what kind of literature you are reading. This has nothing to do with the question of inspiration; it has everything to do with a better understanding of what we are expected to see and hear in its sacred words.

Whenever I am asked what I see as the major teaching of the book of Job, I respond with the tongue-in-cheek: "It makes me pray daily that at those heavenly council meetings my name never comes up!" We are informed that *the sons of God* (the literal Hebrew) come for what we assume is a regular meeting. Along with them comes *The Satan* (in Hebrew *the Accuser*, not a proper name*)*. When God asks what he has been doing, the Accuser replies, "I've been patrolling the earth and checking things out." (Evidently, simply doing what he is expected to do.) It is then that God asks if he has taken note of an exceptionally good man named Job. He has and charges that the only reason Job is such a shining example of righteousness is that God is in the protection racket – he has made Job wealthy and put a hedge around him to shield him from all the bad things in life. "Just take away that hedge and Job will turn on you in an instant," the Accuser smirks.

God insists that Job will maintain his integrity regardless of his circumstances and instigates a contest to prove it by allowing the Accuser to do whatever he chooses to Job, short of taking his life. And so, the game begins with poor Job at home thinking that this will be another good day in God's bright world of blessings. Little does he know how quickly all those blessings are to come tumbling down and leave him sitting in an ash heap with his wife counseling him to curse God and die.

What follows is the arrival of Job's friends and, after seven days of silence, the beginning of the debate. His friends have read the book of Deuteronomy which clearly teaches that the Lord will bless those who serve him with good things and will curse those who do bad things. The withholding of rain and the famine which so often followed are seen as God's judgment on his people for disobeying him (most often it is the sin of idolatry). The lesson is clear: when you do good, good things will come to you; when you do bad, bad things will come to you. (Sounds so much like *the law of attraction* that was made most popular by the recent bestseller *The Secret*.) Job insists that he is innocent of wrongdoing and that what has come upon him is undeserved. His "friends" keep insisting that if he were righteous these bad things would not have happened to him. They know their theology. They know how life works. They know how God works. Case closed.

A young woman once came to me in tears because her baby had died from SIDS and her friends were saying it was God's will. One even declared decisively to her, "God needed your baby more than you did," to which she replied, "Then why did God give her to me in the first place?"

Her friends were no better than Job's friends in offering her bad theology instead of simply weeping with her over her tragic loss. Why do we and other people so often feel that we must give explanations? Could we not rather learn in the face of calamity to grieve over it first and leave the mysteries in God's gracious care?[9]

The book of Job makes for no easy read because Job *does* right and everything *doesn't* turn out okay. He doesn't reap what he has sown. Maintaining his integrity and his faithfulness (he refuses to curse God, although he does curse the day he was born) does not pay dividends. Very bad things happen to a very good person – period. When God finally shows up, after his initial lecturing to Job (which we will explore later), he announces that Job is correct in maintaining his innocence and Job's friends have been mistaken in

9   Dawn, Marva J., *Being Well When We're Ill* (Minneapolis: Augsburg Books, 2008), 72.

their theology – they have been wrong. God then announces that
the only reason he is not going to measure out the harsh judgment
they deserve is that Job is going to pray for them. And the debate
ends with Job praying for those whose efforts at making sense of
life only served to increase his despair.

Another misdirection on the part of the friends is that they
give Job clear, rational, traditional left-brain answers to what is,
basically, not a left-brained question. What is at issue is Job's feelings, not even primarily his physical pain, but his sense of betrayal
by the Friend he has trusted for a lifetime.

What Job yearns for – what the bereaved at a wake or the pa-
tient coming out of the oncologist's office or the deserted spouse
yearns for – is not rational answers but empathy, not only from his
friends, but also from his *Friend*.[10]

The brief epilogue of 42:12-16 at first may appear to resurrect
the philosophy of Deuteronomy with God's restoring more than
Job had before the contest. There is a new family but that could
not have been much comfort to the old family that had been wiped
out and, as we all know, no remaining or new child can "make up"
for one that has been lost. But that is another story. The book
ends with Job's dying *old and full of years*.

The really big question raised by the book of Job is: "Does
God put a protective hedge around those who are his?" (1:10). Are
there bad things that happen to everyone simply because we live
in a world where bad things happen? The light from the book of
Job is the illumination it brings by expanding the dimensions of
the question about bad things happening to good people. In the
remainder of this book we will attempt to look at some of those
added dimensions and explore some of those additional questions.
We not finished with Job. Or should we say, Job is not yet finished
with us!

---

10 O'Malley, William J., The Oldest Question (Chicago: Loyola Press,
    2000), 187.

QUESTIONS FOR REFLECTION AND DISCUSSION

1. How do you read the book of Job in the light of the fact that, just shy of three chapters, the entire book is poetry?
2. Do you believe God ever answers Job's questions? If not, why not, and If so, how does he do it?
3. What are some of the "left-brain answers" you have heard in an attempt to "explain" suffering?
4. How would you answer the question, "Does God put a hedge around those who are his?"
5. How does it change the way you read Job if you accept that it is Job who is on trial and not God?

III BEWARE OF KANGAROO EXEGESIS

Dr. Dale Moody was the first one who introduced me to the phrase "kangaroo exegesis." He maintained that by using this method in Bible reading, one could prove almost anything. The method is simply that one hops around from one verse to another all through the Bible, ignoring the author, purpose of writing, culture, time of writing, etc. It means reading with no regard for context or continuity. It means reading as though Scripture were written in English, only recently, and published by Harper and Row.

> I have said that my master found religious sanction for his cruelty. As an example, I will state one of the many facts going to prove the charge. I have seen him tie up a lame young woman, and whip her with a heavy cowskin upon her naked shoulders, causing the warm red blood to drip; and, in justification of the bloody deed, he would quote this passage of Scripture – "He that knoweth his master's will, and doeth it not, shall be beaten with many stripes" (Luke 12:47).[11]

Real Bible study is hard work because we can't bring intuitively all the necessary background information to enable us to *rightly divide the word of truth* (II Timothy 2:15; KJV). If I don't know who Jeremiah was, when he lived, and what the role of a prophet was, how can I even begin to understand this "weeping prophet"? If I don't know anything about the concept of kinsman redeemer, what can I make of the book of Ruth? Only real study enables me to understand the bold move on the part of Ruth as she lies down

11 Douglass, Frederick, *Narrative of the Life of Frederick Douglass*, 55.

next to Boaz and *uncovers his feet.* This was nothing less than a proposal of marriage in a patriarchal culture that basically viewed and treated women as property. Most of the truly astounding things in Scripture are *not* unearthed by a casual, unstudied approach.

The only way I believe you ever come to the great truths of the Bible is by using as your exegetical principle *the totality of the biblical witness.* It means you always ask not only, "What does this verse of Scripture say to us" but you also ask, "What else does the Bible have to say in other places about this question?"

The division of the biblical text into chapters and verses makes it convenient for location of material but is a major problem evidenced when someone cites a passage with the words, "Verse six tells us...." Separated from the rich context of the remainder of the chapter and the purpose of the book as a whole, we can miss a great deal. I often suggest in workshops that if one wants to come to a richer understanding of the Gospel of Mark, it should be read in its entirety in a single sitting. Then I suggest these questions be asked: "What are the big things that leap out at me from my reading? What are the central teachings that are most apparent? What are the major emphases of the Gospel? What is the big picture of what I have just read?" Reading in totality enables us to get a "feel" for the book as well as a hearing that avoids simply the bits and pieces of lessons and teachings we keep looking for. I maintain that if you want to understand the parts you first must have some understanding of the whole.

I once attended a week-long seminar on the Gospel of Mark. On the concluding evening of the study, our teacher recited the Gospel from memory – without any comment. At the end of his presentation, I turned to my wife and said, "I don't believe I have ever heard that before!" I could not believe the power of his words that transported me back into a time in which the first hearers of the Gospel heard it in just the same way. Many people are taken aback to discover that, first of all, the New Testament was meant to be *heard.* That is why I suggest that even in our private readings, if possible, it brings a new dimension to our understanding when we read aloud.

This same procedure can be used for any other book in the Bible, although the length of some will require breaks in the reading. We all know that the writers did not incorporate chapter and verse divisions into their composition. The scrolls in the synagogue were simply unrolled until the reader found what he was looking for (as we are told Jesus did for his sermon at Nazareth). But the scrolls were the great reminder that the writings were all of one piece.

I grew up in a church that emphasized redemption almost to the exclusion of everything else. Biblically, redemption is not the end of a journey, it is the beginning. To be "saved" is not only to be saved *from* something but, more importantly, to be saved *to* something. The message of both John the Baptist and Jesus begins with the single word "repent." That word often is used in the sense of sorrow and regret instead of its basic meaning of a new direction, a new perspective, a new way to look at life, at new way to live life.

The author of the Epistle of James got under Martin Luther's skin so much that he called the letter "a rather strawy epistle." He couldn't accept the writer's assertion that showing one's faith by action is the antidote to those who simply proclaim their faith without any works to back it up. *The just shall live by faith* (Habakkuk 2:4; Romans 1:17) never meant that works had no role to play in our faith.

Too many have never taken time to notice the way Jesus' Sermon on the Mount (Matthew 5-7) concludes. The sermon, literally a summary of his teachings about what it means to be a disciple, ends with a crash. Reading the sermon at a single sitting with the parable at the end gives one an entirely new perspective on the life of faith. Jesus' parable is about two builders who construct houses in a wadi (a dry river bed). The first builds a solid rock foundation and then puts up the structure. The second builds the house on sand. When the rain, wind, and floods come the first house stands, the second falls *with a great crash* (literal Greek translation).

The key to understanding the parable comes in Jesus words: *Everyone who hears these words of mine and **puts them into practice** is like a wise person who built a house on the rock.... Everyone who hears these words of mine and **does not put them into practice** is like a foolish person who built a house on sand* (with my emphases). My take: Faith which is divorced from action is indeed a sandy faith and faith matched by action is a rock faith. It is important to remember that the wind and flood come to both – life does not spare even the faithful from the storms of life. What is important is that doing what Jesus teaches is the way not to be swept away by life's injustices and tragedies.

> *In the parable of the sheep and goats and the final judgment in Matthew 25:31-46, Jesus doesn't mention a single thing the goats have done wrong! Their crime was their inaction, not their action. (From a chapter entitled: "In God's Eyes, We Are All Action Figures.")*[12]

This is one aspect of changing the question from "Why doesn't God do something?" to "What have I been doing?" This keeps us out of the victim mode even when life hits us with its worst.

QUESTIONS FOR REFLECTION AND DISCUSSION

1. What are some examples of "kangaroo exegesis" that you have heard?
2. How has it changed the way you read a particular text when you made a discovery about the culture or religious life of the context?
3. Why do you believe Jesus concludes the Sermon on the Mount with the parable of the builders?
4. How do you understand the meaning of "the totality of the biblical witness"? What does it do to/for our interpretation of biblical texts?

---

12 Morris, Jonathan, *The Way to Serenity* (New York: HarperCollins, 2014), 123.

5. Have you ever read an entire New Testament book in a single sitting? How did it change what you "heard"?

IV CREATION IS NOT YET FULLY REDEEMED

Nature is our fallen sister, not our mother.[13]

> *Against its will, everything on earth was subjected to God's curse. All creation anticipates the day when it will join God's children in glorious freedom from death and decay. For we know that all creation has been groaning as in the pains of childbirth right up to the present time.* (Romans 8:20-22).

In all the battles between science and religion, one important question is usually overlooked. After settling the matter of the origin of creation, we are faced with the larger issue of just what has made this creation far from what it ought to be. The oft quoted line from Shakespeare, *"The times are out of joint,"* can be cited for almost any time in human history. We seek in vain for a return to the idyllic early life in the Garden of Eden. Those created in the image of God appear not to have been able to maintain the peace and harmony of God's good creation.

In Genesis, we meet temptation in the form of a serpent and wonder why God leaves Adam and Eve unguarded from this talking predator. We immediately sense that there are other forces at work in God's good creation and for some reason he is allowing them free reign. It is evident that a large part of what it means to be

---

13 Yancey, Philip, *Where Is God When It Hurts?* (Grand Rapids: Zondervan, 1990), 61. (From a chapter titled "The Groaning Planet").

created in the image of God is the freedom to make decisions. Volumes have been written on the subject of free-will and just what part it plays in the failure of God's intention for his world. After warning Adam (Eve has not yet appeared on the scene) about the consequences of eating from a certain tree in the garden, God lets the matter rest. He posts no guardian angel or erects a protective fence. The tree and its fruit are readily available for the taking.

All is well until the serpent questions Eve about the restrictions God has established. The serpent maintains that God is holding out on Adam and Eve and that the reason he has forbidden them to eat of this one tree is that he doesn't want them to know too much – he doesn't want them to know what he knows. However, one reads this, as an attempt to assert independence from God or simply the desire to satisfy the natural desire for knowledge, the meaning is all the same – Adam and Eve want to change the relationship between creatures and Creator. They no longer want to be number two; perhaps they just want to be number one-and-a-half. It's probably too much to suggest that they want to be God; they certainly want to be more like him.

The Christian understanding of this story is repeated in the Gospels when Jesus meets the same kind of temptation, now in the form of a personified Satan. He refuses to abdicate his role as a faithful son to the Heavenly Father and turns down Satan's offer of a powerful earthly kingdom all his own (if he could have delivered it is still a question). The writer of Ephesians goes a step further:

> *For our struggle is not against flesh and blood, but against the rulers, against the authorities, against the powers of this dark world and against the spiritual forces of evil in the heavenly realms. 6:12.*

The Bible acknowledges not only evil as a force in the world but expands it into cosmic proportions. Not until we get to the book of Revelation do we find any resolution of the problem of evil in all of its dimensions.

As I write these lines I am in the process of reading *Auschwitz: A New History* by Lawrence Rees.[14]   The cover has these words above the title: *How Mankind Committed the Ultimate Infamy.* The dedication page reads: "In memory of the 1.1 million men, women and children who died at Auschwitz." The section I just completed concerns the plight of the Slovakian Jews. The authorities constructed "The Little Red House" some distance from the main facility and gassed the victims at night so the rest of those in the camp could not hear the screams of the dying. At the burning bush, God tells Moses: *I have indeed seen the misery of my people in Egypt, I have heard them crying out because of their slave drivers, and I am concerned about their suffering.* (Exodus 3:7). Did God not see the misery of those at Auschwitz, did he not hear their screams; was he not concerned about their suffering? Why didn't God do something about this? These are not only Jewish questions, they are questions for all of us as we struggle with the horror of this kind of evil.

"Does God's gift of freedom extend to our being able to unleash unbelievable destruction and death on masses of humanity? It would seem so." Are you shocked by this idea? It shocks me. In his introduction to *Auschwitz*, Rees concludes: "In this history, suffering is almost never redemptive. Although there are, on very rare occasions, extraordinary people who act virtuously, for the most part this is a story of degradation."[15] Someone said to me in an attempt to allay my worry over a situation, "There's no need to worry. God is still in charge. Everything is going to be okay." Those being shoved into the gas chambers at Auschwitz wouldn't have bought that. Neither do I. Sometimes it does not appear that God is in charge. Sometimes everything does not turn out okay.

Perhaps one of the most disturbing assumptions in the Old Testament is that God is the author of the bad as well as the good.

The reason for the paucity of references to Satan in the Old Testament is that in the Old Testament it was Yahweh himself who

---

14 Lawrence Rees, *A New History* (New York: MJF Books, 2005).
15 Ibid, xix.

was responsible for evil, so the figure of a devil was not necessary. Amos 3:6 (KJV) Shall there be evil in a city, and the Lord hath not done it? Isaiah 45:5-7 (KJV) I am the Lord, and there is none else…. I form the light, and create darkness: I make peace, and create evil; I the Lord do all these things. Isaiah 54:7 I create the blacksmith, who builds a fire and forges weapons. I also create the soldier, who uses the weapons to kill.[16]

John Wesley published a sermon in 1750, "The Cause and Cure of Earthquakes," in which he affirms that they are a sign of God's anger against sin.[17]

My daughter at about six years of age asked me the question, "Why do we speak of the good Lord?" Whereupon I said, "Some weeks ago, you were suffering from measles, and then, the good Lord sent you full recovery." However, the little girl was not content but she returned, "Well; but, please, Daddy, do not forget: in the first place, he had sent me the measles."[18]

QUESTIONS FOR REFLECTION AND DISCUSSION

1. What is your initial reaction to the idea that we are living in a world that is not yet fully redeemed?
2. How do you interpret the presence of the serpent in the Garden of Eden?
3. Why do you believe God did not post a guardian angel around the Tree of Knowledge in the Garden?
4. How far do you believe God's gift of freedom for us to choose extends? All the way to Auschwitz?

---

16 John A. Sanford, *The Shadow Side of Reality* (New York: Crossroad 1984), 26-26.
17 Leslie D. Weatherhead, *Why Do Men Suffer?* (New York: Abingdon-Cokesbury Press 1936), 65.
18 Victor E. Frankl, *Man's Search for Meaning* (Boston: Beacon Press, 1959), 120-121.

5. How do you interpret the cited Old Testament passages about God being responsible for evil? Do you believe he sends earthquakes and the measles?

V BEGINNING WITH GOD'S LOVE INSTEAD OF HIS SOVEREIGNTY

Though my personal faith has been stretched by many difficult questions and the old traditional answers have been deeply challenged by suffering, and though I have questions and yelled at God in my darkest hours, I know God's love for me. I have never been alone.[19]

With all the lamenting and complaining we cited in chapter two, Psalms sounds a major note along with much in a minor key: God's everlasting love – *Give thanks to the Lord, for he is good; his love endures forever* (Psalm 107:1). Psalm 118 opens with the same phrase. In Psalm 136, a responsive liturgy used in worship, the congregation repeats the phrase, *His love endures forever,* twenty-six times! This is surely intended to be made a mind and faith imprint.

In most discussions about predestination (we will touch on this later), those who are threatened by too much "free will" talk, come down hard on God's sovereignty and attempt to prove that his power overrides those who plan to do something that is against his purpose and plan. I simply will never believe that Auschwitz had any place in God's plan. I don't believe Hitler had any place in God's purpose and plan. And, yet, he allowed those who planned what has rightly been called the most evil regime in the history of the world to have their way. He did not use his power to stop them.

Rabbi Kushner is one of my favorite authors and his *When Bad Things Happen to Good People*[20] remains one of my recom-

---

19 Herman, Doug, *What Good is God?*, 30.
20 Harold S. Kushner, *When Bad Things Happen to Good People* (New York: Shocken Books, 1981).

mendations. This is not an abstract book about God and theology but resulted from the news that his three-year-old son's diagnosis of progeria (rapid aging) would cause him to die in his early teens. This is an honest, thoughtful, must read for all who struggle with how God as an all-wise, all-powerful parent can allow things like this to happen – especially for people who are doing all they can to be good people. Many are shocked that Rabbi Kushner's conclusion is that God does not act on such occasions, not because he lacks love, but because he lacks the ability to do so - God is limited in what he can do. Some pitch a fit over this "solution," but for Kushner, and many others, it is a logical answer to the question of why God doesn't do what we know an all-powerful God can and should do.

What is important to note is that we find in Kushner's book the same thing we find in the psalms – there is never an abandonment of belief in God. Here is his unique observation on prayer which I have found very helpful:

> *In your desperation, you opened your heart in prayer, and what happened? You didn't get a miracle to avert a tragedy. But you discovered people around you, and God beside you, and strength within you to help you survive the tragedy. I offer this as an example of a prayer being answered.*[21]

In 1982, Kushner reported that about ten percent of the calls and letters he's received since the books release were from fundamentalists trying to convert him. What I find most revealing is that two-thirds were from people thanking him and saying things like, "For the first time in ten years I go to church again. It's very sustaining."[22]

I suspect the return has everything to do with their discovery of God's love, mercy, and grace (from many sources) and very little to do with the reassurance of his all-powerful status. I believe the often quoted "Nothing is impossible with God" is certainly true as long as you take this to mean everything that is a part of his ul-

21 Ibid, 131.
22 Carol Krucoff, Article in *The Washington Post.* January 2, 1982.

timate purpose and plan for his world. What is impossible is that which is contrary to his nature, contrary to his love, and contrary to any violation of the gift of freedom he has given to those he created in his own image.

Nothing is impossible with God does not mean that we should be able to persuade him to do whatever we want in making things right in our lives and our world. The offerings to idols in the pagan world were usually the attempt to persuade their gods to intervene on their behalf in a certain situation. It was essentially a bribe. The formula for praying Jesus gives in the Sermon on the Mount is simply to bring requests in few and simple words to a Father who loves his children more than we can imagine and then trust (leave the matter at that). We are warned that "much speaking" does not persuade God to hear us better. We already have his ear and we are already in his care (as are the birds of the air and the flowers of the field).

The emphasis everywhere in Scripture is on God's grace, mercy, and love. Although we believe *God is able to do abundantly above all that we ask or think,* the place to begin in thinking about God is most pointedly given in John 3:16: *For God so loved the world that he gave....* Having questions about God's failure to act when we are praying and crying our eyes out does not mean that God has ceased to love us. Even in their laments the psalmists never equated the two, although at times they did wonder where he was.

> *The terror of sickness and old age is not merely the terror of the losses one is forced to endure but also the terror of the isolation.*[23]

I may not understand what is happening to me and those I care about and why God doesn't do something, but that does not mean that I have any reason to believe that he has abandoned me. Romans 8:35-39 is the great reminder of what can (and does) happen to God's people and where we stand in the middle of it all:

---

23 Atul Gawande, *Being Mortal* (New York: Metropolitan Books, 2014), 146.

*Who shall separate us from the love of Christ? Shall trouble
or hardship or persecution or famine or nakedness or danger or
sword? As it is written: "For your sake we face death all day long;
we are considered as sheep to be slaughtered." No, in all these
things we are more than conquerors through him who loved us.
For I am convinced that neither death nor life, neither angels nor
demons, neither the present nor the future, nor any powers, neither
height nor depth, nor anything else in all creation, will be able to
separate us from the love of God that is in Christ Jesus our Lord.*

Paul begins and ends where we should – with God's love.

It has been many years since I read Corrie ten Boom's *The
Hiding Place* and later saw the movie. The one line from both the
book and the movie that I have never forgotten is: "However deep
the pit, God's love is deeper still." What makes the statement so
memorable is that it comes from one who was in the deep pit of a
Nazi death camp. I cannot imagine how it could get much deeper
than that.

QUESTIONS FOR REFLECTION AND DISCUSSION

1. Why do you think so many are concerned about God's
   sovereignty? Do you believe there are things that happen
   outside of God's will?
2. What does the phrase "Nothing is impossible with God" mean
   to you?
3. What do you believe was the purpose of the writer in Psalm
   136?
4. How do you respond to Kushner's conclusion that the reason
   God does not act in certain situations is not a lack of love but
   the lack of ability?
5. How do you feel about Paul's contention in Romans 8 that,
   even though God may never prevent some terrible things
   happening to us, he never abandons us, he never allows
   anything to distance us from his love?

VI Our Limited Perspective

If we really let God be God, the Sovereign Lord of the cosmos, he will be too vast and mysterious for us ever to be comfortable.[24]

If God's questioning of Job does anything, it reminds him how much he doesn't know (Job 38:1f.):

> *Then the Lord spoke to Job out of the storm. He said: "Who is this that obscures my plans with words without knowledge? Prepare to defend yourself; I will question you, and you shall answer me."*

> *"Where were you when I laid the earth's foundation? ... Who marked off its dimensions?" (v. 4-5)*

> *"Have you ever given orders to the morning, or shown the dawn its place?" (v. 12)*

> *"Have the gates of death been shown to you?" (v.17)*

> *"Have you comprehended the vast expanses of the earth?" (v. 18)*

> *"What is the way to the abode of light? And where does darkness reside?" (v. 19)*

---

24 Dawn, Marva J., *Being Well When We're Ill*, 84.

Paul's famous *"We see dimly in a mirror"* challenges us to consider that even what we do see is distorted. Nothing we ever see is viewed with total clarity. The often quoted, "I have a point of view, you have a point of view, only God has view," gives the same word of caution when we are tempted to speak with too much authority and finality. "Subject to change without notice" is true of much more than the political pronouncements that assail us during election campaigns. Everything is not tentative, to be sure, but almost everything needs adjustments in the light of additional information, new insights, and the greater understanding of life's complexities that come with additional life-experiences.

> *Before I continue my personal story, let me give you some idea of where I'm heading. It's all about control. Control is illusory. No matter what university you go to, no matter what degree you hold, if your goal is to become master of your own destiny you have more to learn. Parkinson's is a perfect metaphor for lack of control.*[25]

The most disturbing words that confront those who want to live by easy and simplistic assurances, serenity, and security are: mystery, paradox, and ambiguity. I maintain that if these three words are not a part of your understanding of life – and of faith – that you will never be blessed with any large measure of the gift of peace Jesus promised his followers. These three words are reminders that many things that happen in life are beyond explanations or solutions. There is no available tree of knowledge whose fruits will enable us to be god-like in knowing and understanding. There is nothing that can lift us from humanity to divinity. There is nothing that will enable us to know as God knows.

> *We ourselves are the strongest argument against our own doubts. We do not wait until the meaning of everything is made plain before doing anything. We operate on the basis of partial*

---

25 Fox, Michael J., *A Funny Thing Happened On the Way to the Future*, 84.

and fragmentary insights which give us enough light to go on for the moment.[26]

It is not a matter of asking whether or not we can live with unanswered questions. If we choose to go on living after some tragedy, we must. One of the lines I use in workshops is: "You don't have to have all your questions answered to move forward in life. You can live with unanswered questions." Most people know that their question "Why?" cannot be answered.

Sitting with a grieving family the day following the death of their son in an automobile accident on the Blue Ridge Parkway, I heard the father ask that question a dozen times followed by his lament, "What a waste!" The eighteen year old son, the night before his high school graduation, had taken a friend to the nearby mountains to find out how many stations his new FM car radio could pick up. They never returned. The car was found at 3:00 a.m. down a mountain side smashed against a tree. The friend had survived, the driver did not. The only fact in the accident was gravel on the curve where the car went off the road. The source of that gravel remains unknown. The police suspect that the tires could not maintain traction when they hit that gravel and the car slid off the road. That is probably what happened; no one would even attempt to suggest why it happened.

I often ask in situations like this: *if* there were an answer to why it happened, would this offer any satisfaction or resolution? I don't believe it would. Rational answers do very little to speak to emotional questions. This family was spared from any who dared to utter the heartless: "God must have some reason for this that we do not know. We simply have to trust that God never makes mistakes." Such attempts at comfort (which I continue to hear uttered) leave me shaking my head. Jesus never gave anyone he met a "reason" for the infirmity that was crippling their lives. Jesus had no response to either Martha or Mary when they said, "If you had been here our brother would not have died." The text tells us

26 Holloway, Richard, *Paradoxes of Christian Faith and Life* (Oxford: Mowbray, 1984), 27.

he stood by the grave of Lazarus and *burst into tears* (John 11:35
- the literal Greek).

That was the only "answer" he had to their grief. It is a mis-
take to rush too quickly to Jesus words "*Lazarus, come forth!*" and
ignore the sorrow and pain that come with the loss of a loved one.
Nowhere in Scripture is lament a neglected or forgotten word. This
has nothing to do with a lack of faith or of the hope of resurrection
we believe lies at the center of our faith. Thankfully, no one robbed
Pat and me of our need to grieve the loss and feel the pain in the
death of our son. Nothing anyone could have said would have
made it "easier" or enabled us to say, "Now we understand it so
much better." Neither of us needed "answers"; we simply needed
people to stand with us in our grief – and remain with us as long as
it took for us to be able to inch our feet out the door into life again.

In commenting on John 9:3, Jesus' encounter with the man
born blind and the question from his disciples, Marva Dawn writes:

> *The proper question is not "Who is to blame?" but "What*
> *good might God reveal through this affliction?" – and the answer to*
> *that question might not even be known in this life. It is a mystery*
> *that we will only fully understand at the end of time.*[27]

QUESTIONS FOR REFLECTION AND DISCUSSION

1. Do you believe Marva Dawn is correct when she writes that
   "God is too vast and mysterious for us ever to be comfortable"?
2. Where have you learned in your life that control is illusory?
3. Do you have a problem with allowing mystery, paradox, and
   ambiguity to be a part of life *and* faith?
4. When are the times in your life that you were able to get on
   with life despite unanswered questions?
5. What would you have said to the family whose son was killed
   in an automobile accident on the Blue Ridge Parkway?

---

27 Dawn, 67.

VII IS IT POSSIBLE TO SING THE LORD'S SONG IN A STRANGE LAND?

We were up against the unfixable. But we were desperate to believe that we weren't up against the unmanageable .... He found that in the narrow space of possibility that his awful tumor had left for him there was still room to live.[28]

The response of the Israelites to their captors in Babylon is understandable; it is also the response many of us make when we find ourselves in a place where the people we have lost and the things we have loved are lost to another place and another time. When the "tormentors" demand "songs of joy" (Psalm 137:3), what they get in return is a lament: *How can we sing the songs of the Lord while in a strange land?* (Psalm 137:4). Their response/question has many dimensions: "How can we be happy now that everything that once made us happy as God's people is gone? Wouldn't it be hypocritical to sing one of Temple songs in a place where we see only temples to pagan gods? Isn't what you are asking us to do a betrayal of our faith and our heritage and our God? Isn't what you are asking us to do a denial of our present situation?"

... one of the greatest truths in the world: that what happens to us doesn't matter vitally. The only thing that really matters is what happens in us.[29]

The decision had really been made prior to the request: *By the rivers of Babylon we sat and wept when we remembered Zion. There on the poplars we hung our harps* (Psalm 137:1-2). They were

---

28 Gawande, Atul, *Being Mortal,* 223, 229.
29 Weatherhead, Leslie D., *Why Do Men Suffer?* 31.

in grief and it probably was a time for weeping – and a time for remembering Zion. The hanging of the harps on poplar or willow trees (either translation is possible) is understandable – as long as it was not meant to be a permanent installation! Were the people saying, "We will *never* be able to sing the Lord's songs in Babylon!"? Jeremiah's counsel certainly came as a shocking "corrective" to the perpetual stance of "conquered" that many wanted to adopt.

Here is the advice he gives to those whose harps and voices have gone into remission (Jeremiah 29:4-7):

> *This is what the Lord Almighty, the God of Israel, says to all those I carried into exile from Jerusalem to Babylon: "Build houses and settle down; plant gardens and eat what they produce. Marry and have sons and daughters; find wives for your sons and give your daughters in marriage, so that they too may have sons and daughters. Increase in number there; do not decrease. Also, seek the peace and prosperity of the city to which I have carried you into exile. Pray to the Lord for it, because if it prospers, you too will prosper."*

You begin to understand just how much this advice was needed when you read the last two verses of Psalm 137: *Daughter Babylon, doomed to destruction, happy are those who repay you according to what you have done to us. Happy are those who seize your infants and dash them against the rocks.* This is a shocking retribution to most modern readers but would have been easily understood in the culture of that day. While the desire for payback is the natural response to what happened, if one lives only for revenge the possibilities for a productive and happy life are reduced to practically zero. Jeremiah is giving the prescription for life, even in Babylon.

"We'll sing the Lord's song when we get back home again," must have been the answer most wanted to give to the taunting request. But home was never going to be same again. The Temple was in ruins and the city had already begun to be populated with other "kinds" of people. The Jerusalem of old was no more; it was gone forever. Many years later when there was a return of some of the exiles (many chose to remain in Babylon), it was no easy matter to rebuild the wall and restore some of the joy of the Lord's song in their own land.

> *We who lived in concentration camps can remember the men who walked through the huts comforting others, giving away their last piece of bread. They may have been few in number, but they offer sufficient proof that everything can be taken from a man but one thing: the last of the human freedoms – to choose one's attitude in any given set of circumstances, to choose one's own way ....*
> *And there were always choices to make.*[30]

The question put to the captives resurfaced in the twentieth century in a place that makes Babylon look like the Garden of Eden. Victor Frankl had a Jeremiah like message for his fellow prisoners in Auschwitz: "It is possible to sing the Lord's song even in a place that seems like hell." His classic book, *Man's Search for Meaning*, describes the horror of the Holocaust in vivid detail and the courage and heroism of many who were its victims. Frankl gives some of the most unbelievable advice and suggested strategies you will ever read.

> *The attempt to develop a sense of humor and to see things in a humorous light is some kind of a trick learned while mastering the art of living. Yet it is possible to practice the art of living even in a concentration camp, although suffering is omnipresent.*

> *(We found ourselves) grateful for the smallest of mercies. We were glad for a time to delouse before going to bed. If we could not do the job properly we were kept awake half the night.* [31]

---

30 Frankl, Victor, *Man's Search for Meaning*, 157.
31 Ibid, 43, 46.

QUESTIONS FOR REFLECTION AND DISCUSSION

1. What are some of the "strange lands" in which you have found yourself and yet were able, at least to some degree, to sing the Lord's song?
2. When are some of the times in your life that you have "hung your harp on a weeping willow tree"?
3. How do you think Jeremiah's advice to the exiles in Babylon applies to us?
4. What is your response to the last verses of Psalm 137? Were you surprised to discover them in a psalm?
5. What do you think of Victor Frankl's counsel to the prisoners in the Nazi concentration camps?

VIII WHAT WOULD MOSES, GIDEON, AND JESUS SAY TO US?

John Henry Newman:

> *"God has created me to do for Him some definite service;*
> *He has committed some work to me which He has not committed*
> *to another. I have my mission .... Somehow, I am necessary for*
> *His purposes, as necessary in my place as an Archangel in his."*[32]

Not all Scripture is easily understood and interpreted in the same way by all who read it. Some texts are fairly murky and others lend themselves to distortion suited to one's purpose. Note this warning in 2 Peter 3:16: *(Paul's) letters contain some things that are hard to understand, which ignorant and unstable people distort, as they do the other Scriptures, to their own destruction.* That is why it is always important to begin with Scriptures that, according to most interpreters, are perfectly clear in what they teach. Three such texts are the basis of our thinking for this chapter:

> *The Lord said, "I have indeed seen the misery of my people in Egypt. I have heard them crying because of their slave drivers, and I am concerned about their suffering. So I have come down to rescue them....SO NOW I AM SENDING YOU TO PHARAOH TO BRING MY PEOPLE THE ISRAELITES OUT OF EGYPT.*
> *(Exodus 3:7, 8,10 emphasis mine.)*

> *When the angel of the Lord appeared to Gideon he said, "The Lord is with you, mighty*

---

32 Morris, Jonathan, *The Way to Serenity*, 119.

> warrior." "Pardon me, my lord," Gideon replied,
> but if the Lord is with us, why has all this hap-
> pened to us? Where are all his wonders that
> our ancestors told us about when they said, 'Did
> not the Lord bring us up out of Egypt?' But now
> the Lord has abandoned us and given us into
> the hands of Midian." The Lord turned to him
> and said, "GO IN THE STRENGTH YOU HAVE AND
> SAVE ISRAEL OUT OF MIDIAN'S HAND. AM I
> NOT SENDING YOU?"
> (Judges 6:12-14. Emphasis mine.)

> As he went along, he saw a man blind
> from birth. His disciples asked him, "Rabbi, who
> sinned, this man or his parents, that he was
> born blind?" "Neither this man nor his parents
> sinned," said Jesus, "BUT THIS HAS HAPPENED
> SO THAT THE WORKS OF GOD MIGHT BE DIS-
> PLAYED IN HIM." (John 9:1-3 – emphasis mine.
> I interrupt this last verse to mean: "This man's
> blindness is not the result of anyone's sin, but I
> will use his blindness as an occasion for demon-
> strating the grace and mercy of God.")

In response to the question "Why doesn't God do something?" in these three situations we are told God *is* going to do something. He is going to do something by using people to carry out his will and purpose. In the first two instances, both Moses and Gideon come up with a myriad of excuses as to why they are not qualified for the job. Only Jesus immediately steps up to act. In the face of tragedy, suffering, and injustice the immediate questions for all of us are: "What can I do about this? How can I act compassionately and redemptively in this situation? What is my role as one of God's instruments in his world to help his will be done on earth as it is in heaven." This last question comes from a prayer (The Lord's Prayer) that most of us make on a fairly regular basis, hardly imagining the role we are called to play in bringing some of it about.

When I think that these precious souls are today shut up in the prison-house of slavery, my feelings overcome me, and I am almost ready to ask, "Does a righteous God govern the universe? And for what end does he hold the thunders in his right hand, if not to smite the oppressor, and deliver the spoiled out of the hand of the spoiler?"

Baffled, entangled, and discouraged, I had at times asked myself the question, May not my condition after all be God's work, and ordered for a wise purpose, and if so, is not submission my duty?[33]

To the immediate plea "Let us pray!" in the light of tragedy, the Bible adds the command, "Let us act!" It is not a call to reverse whatever catastrophe has come (which is usually impossible) but to find something we can do to make a difference in the lives of those who have been affected. And I maintain there is *always something* we can do. Our actions and the results will not be as spectacular as that achieved by Moses, Gideon, and Jesus but they will be our part in God's doing something.

It is extremely noteworthy that Jesus did not explain the blindness that had afflicted the man since birth. When the disciples asked if it could be the result of the man's own sin, this reflects a current idea that if parents were righteous beyond question, then it could only be that the child sinned while still in his mother's womb! To us this idea seems incredible, but is no more farfetched than the lengths to which some will go to explain the cause of sickness. Jesus was short on explanation and long on action. He refused to waste time on the "Why?" and immediately moved to "What?" – What can be done to help this man in his sightless condition?

It is amazing how much biblical teaching has to do with actions instead of feelings. Paul's famous chapter on love in 1 Corinthians 13 does not contain a single adjective in describing love. Love is characterized by what it does, not by how it feels. Whenever I use this in wedding ceremonies, I stress to the couple that the commit-

33 Douglass, Frederick, *Narrative of the Life of Frederick Douglass*, 73, 113.

ment they are pledging to each other has to do with a love that can be consistent through all the ups and downs of marriage because it not based on how they feel but on how they decide to act.

The three texts at the beginning of this chapter highlight an almost forgotten word that needs to be resurrected. Each of the individuals had a special calling. That seems evident to most people. The larger truth, expanded in many places in Scripture, is that *everyone* has a calling; we are all among the called. Paul tries to spell that out for some church folks who are hung up on the great "gifts" and seem to be overlooking the "lesser gifts." His message is clear: there are no lesser gifts and there are no lesser callings. If it is your calling, in your particular situation, with the strengths (and weaknesses) that you have, then it is a Divine calling – and it is the one for which you will be held accountable. Jesus warned us not to be like the person who buried his "one" gift in the ground because he feared he might lose that if he attempted to invest it. He is labeled as unfaithful, not because he didn't have great gifts to use, but because he failed to use what had been entrusted to him (Matthew 25:14-30).

> So, if our role is important, one of life's principal tasks is to find out what that role is. The funny thing is, God rarely reveals it all at once. Our role unfolds like chapters in a novel, with all sorts of unexpected plot twists .... Sometimes just doing what we are supposed to be doing is the surest way of fulfilling our mission. [34]

QUESTIONS FOR REFLECTION AND DISCUSSION

1. What do you see as the central message in the three texts at the beginning of this chapter?
2. What has happened when you changed the question from "Why?" to "What?" in the face of some loss or tragedy?
3. What are the times in which the situation changed for you from "Let us pray" to "Let us act"?

---

34 Morris, 120-121.

4. What difference does it make that the description of love in I Corinthians is based on verbs and not adjectives?

5. How does it change our lives when we believe that we *all* have a calling?

IX WHAT DOES IT MEAN TO WALK BY FAITH AND NOT BY SIGHT?

Romans 5:4 – Suffering produces perseverance; perseverance, character, character, hope." Paul lists hope at the end, instead of where I would normally expect it at the beginning, as the fuel that keeps a person going. No, hope emerges from the struggle.[35]

If you want to begin to understand 2 Corinthians 5:7, *We live by faith, not by sight,* it must never be taken as our watchword out of context. It is most instructive to begin reading with 2 Corinthians 4:16-5:1:

> *Therefore, we do not lose heart. Though outwardly we are wasting away, yet inwardly we are being renewed day by day. For our light and momentary afflictions are achieving for us an eternal glory that far outweighs them all. So we fix our eyes not on what is seen, but on what is unseen, since what is seen is temporary, but what is unseen is eternal. For we know that if the earthly tent we live in is destroyed, we have a building from God, an eternal house in heaven, not built by human hands.*

In this "enlightened" age of information overload, and especially with the publication of Ernest Becker's *The Denial of Death* in 1973,[36] you would think a book like *Being Mortal* would hardly be necessary. Yet it remains true that the majority seem to go about their daily affairs with little thought of the limitations our human-

---

35 Herman, Doug, *What Good is God?*, 72.
36 Becker, Ernest, *The Denial of Death* (New York: The Free Press, 1973).

ity has placed on us. It is difficult for most of us to contemplate that tomorrow may *not* be another day. Death is still the forbidden subject and the aging that inevitably comes with being mortal we hope to keep tucked away in special facilities.

Paul writes plainly about how aging is like a "wasting away" and that one day the tent in which we live will be taken down; we will die. No cure has been found for aging, although its effects vary greatly for a multitude of reasons. Atul Gawande in *Being Mortal* describes the present problem in a culture with an ever increasing number of elderly:

> Mainstream doctors are turned off by geriatrics, and that's because they do not have the faculties to cope with the Old Crock," Felix Silverstone, the geriatrician, explained to me. "The Old Crock is deaf. The Old Crock has poor vision. The Old Crock's memory might be somewhat impaired. With the Old Crock, you have to slow down, because he asks you to repeat what you are saying or asking. And the Old Crock doesn't just have a chief complaint – the Old Crock has fifteen chief complaints. How in the world are you going to cope with all of them? You're over-whelmed."[37]

Wasting away has never been better described! And ultimately, the waste is final. But Paul asks us to keep our eyes focused, not on the temporary, but on the eternal. This is not meant to negate wise health care as we age (about which Gawande has many amazing suggestions) or to minimize this life and with its challenges, responsibilities, and joys. This is not an "other worldly" approach to life. Many have observed that those who were most certain of a life hereafter were those who were most interested in caring for the sick and erecting hospitals. Jesus announced that he had come to bring life and stressed that the gift of eternal life begins now!

> *Robert Ellsberg speaking of Dorothy Day:*
>
> "She read the news in the light of eternity."[38]

---

37 Gawande, Atul, *Being Mortal*, 36-37.
38 Wicks, Robert, *No Problem* (Notre Dame: Sorin Books, 2014), 9.

What follows Paul's call to walk by faith and not by sight is a lengthy call to participate in what God is calling us to do in this world at this time. The implication of what he writes is that one day a prayer for healing will *not* be answered. One day our loved ones will slip away from us. One day this life as we know it will be over. But this does not mean that God has abandoned or forgotten us. In fact, he has something *better* planned.

> *God never wills evil; he didn't cause Thom's accident. But he does allow us to pass through a very imperfect world where the laws of fallen nature and abuse of free will wreak havoc on the righteous and evil alike. What we do with our trials depends on us. Whether we choose to live in bitterness and resentment or trust God's providential care depends on us. And in play is that choice to reject or accept the things we cannot change is our serenity of soul.[39]*

Chapter eleven of the book of Hebrews gives what is termed "The Roll Call of Faith." The chapter begins with a definition of faith: *Now faith is being sure of what we hope for and certain of what we do not see* (11:1). This is trust that God will deliver on his promises. After listing such biblical heroes as Abel, Enoch, Noah, Abraham, Sarah, Isaac, Jacob, and Moses, the author then writes that there is not time to tell about the others (vs.32). But he does tell us about a large anonymous number *who were tortured, put to death by stoning, sawed in two, killed by the sword, destitute, persecuted and mistreated.* Verse 38 gives their obituary: *The world was not worthy of them.*

> *What people don't realize is how much religion costs. They think faith is a big electric blanket, when of course it is the cross. It is much harder to believe than not to believe.*

> *Whatever you do anyway, remember that these things are mysteries and that if they were such that we could understand them, they wouldn't be worth understanding. A God you understood would be less than yourself.*

---

39 Morris, Robert, *The Way to Serenity*, 63.

You arrive at enough certainty to be able to make your way, but it is making it in the darkness. Don't expect faith to clear things up for you. It is trust, not certainty.[40]

In Hebrews 11, the people who suffered so terribly were all people of faith, of hope and trust in the goodness and mercy of God. Where was he in their lives to prevent such persecution and mistreatment? In that day, it was one's confession of faith that put one in harm's way. Walking by faith was not the way of easy answers and a hedge of protection. Faith meant having reality vision for this life and an eternal vision for what is above and beyond this life and this world. It meant living life fully but with the eye of faith-vision on eternity.

All these people were still living by faith when they died. They did not receive the things promised: they only saw them and welcomed them from a distance, admitting that they were foreigners and strangers on earth.
— Hebrews 11:13

We are pilgrims passing through a foreign land. Our true homeland lies beyond this life. Most Christians believe this, but rarely live it.[41]

The Bible has two great bookends. The first is the book of Genesis which opens with: *In the beginning God.* The last book in the Bible, Revelation, concludes with: *in the end, God.* Genesis begins with our world being made, Revelation promises a new heaven and a new earth – a new creation. It proclaims: God is finally going to do something on such a grand scale that it will take your breath away! He's going to provide such things that our eyes have never seen and in our wildest imagination we have never conceived (Isaiah 64:4; I Corinthians 2:9) that we probably will find our questions irrelevant.

---

40 Dawn, Marva J., *Being Well When We're Ill*, 31.
41 Morris, 228.

This world is not fair, final, or finished. The biblical message is that things are not going to be "straightened out" until the final wrap-up. This is not "pie in the sky by and by" but the promise of the final redemption of the entire created order and the reward and recognition of "good and faithful servants" (Matthew 25:21).

Patience also means the ability to wait…. The Lord is not a God of quick fixes and the fifteen-minute spiritual oil-changes, but a God of long-term and indeed eternal promises.[42]

QUESTIONS FOR REFLECTION AND DISCUSSION

1. How does it change the concept of faith for you when you read 2 Corinthians 4:16 to 5:1 *before* reading 2 Corinthians 5:7?
2. Have you heard a discussion among your friends about any book like *Being Mortal?* Why do you think this is so?
3. Why do you believe so many doctors are turned off by geriatrics?
4. How does it affect your reading of Scripture to see Genesis and Revelation as the two great bookends?
5. What is your response to the quotation from Jonathan Morris at the end of this chapter?

---

42 Ibid, 32-33.

Is There A More Relevant Question?

There is a German word, durchleiden, for which there is no good English translation. It means to experience and get to know something by suffering. To "suffer a thing through" with your entire being, rather than trying to "figure it out."[43]

> It was good for me to be afflicted so that I might learn your decrees. (Psalm 119:71).

> It was good for me to have to suffer, the better to learn your statutes.
> (Psalm 119:71 – JB).

The problem with continuing to ask the eternal question is that, as of this moment, no one has come up with the "answer." So many factors come to play in seeking to explain how a truly good and loving God who is unlimited in his power (the stance of most believers) can sit idly by while suffering and atrocities abound in his world. Some have found an answer for themselves and those with whom they are associated, but the vast majority of people continue to find the question unanswerable.

I can almost guarantee that most are not going to like what I consider to be a more relevant question (taking into consideration all its ramifications): Is this world a vale of soul-making? The question was first posed by John Keats.

---

43 Herman, Doug, *What Good is God?* 56.

The phrase "the vale of soul-making" was coined by the poet John Keats in a letter written to his brother and sister in April 1819.

> *This world must be a place of soul-making. And its value is to be judged, not primarily by the quality of pleasure and pain occurring in it at any particular moment, but by its fitness for its primary purpose, the purpose of soul-making.*[44]

In our personal lives the question needs to be asked: Where do we learn the most? Michael J. Fox in *A Funny Thing Happened on the way to the Future* puts it bluntly:

> *It may seem hard to believe, but it's catastrophe that offers the most promise for an even richer life. This is the gateway to the good stuff. In other words, you never truly know which way the wind is blowing until the **** hits the fan.*[45]

Other questions to consider are: What does it mean to become the best version of ourselves? How is this accomplished? What about Hebrews 5:8 – *Son though he was, he learned obedience from what he suffered and, once made perfect, he became the source of eternal salvation for all who obey him....*

> *The spiritual practice of recognizing that Jesus called us to take our cross (and not our teddy bear!) enables us to live with the uncertainty of abiding in faith .... Perhaps you can find this text (Mark 8:34) salutary for being well the next time you are tested by the apparent meaningless of your sufferings.*[46]

We have already looked at Paul's list of what *could* come as a result of suffering: *Not only so, but we also glory in our sufferings, because we know that suffering produces perseverance; perseverance, character, and character hope* (Romans 5:4).

Peter Kreeft gives a famous quote from C.S. Lewis but replaces one word with another: "God whispers in our pleasures but shouts

---

44 Hick, John, *Evil and the Love of God*, 259.
45 Fox, Michael J., *A Funny Thing Happened on the Way to the Future*, 80-81.
46 Dawn, Marva J., *Being Well When We're Ill*, 50.

in our pains. Pain is his megaphone to rouse a *dulled* world."[47] The correct version is: "Pain is his megaphone to rouse a *deaf* world." Lewis did not believe the world is simply dulled; he believed the world is deaf when it comes to hearing God's whispers.

I am not saying that any of the suffering and tragedy is inherently good – it can easily devastate and destroy lives. Also, if we do believe this world is a vale of soul-making, this never means that we should ever sit idly by and let injustice and horror roll over the land.

I don't for a moment believe that God sends any of this injustice and horror!!! I fully agree with James 1:17 – *Every good and perfect gift is from above, coming down from the Father of the heavenly lights, who does not change like the shifting shadows ...* We cannot escape the fact, however, that even if God is not the author of such pain, he does allow it to happen.

A good place to begin is with what the Scriptures tell us is the clearest and surest revelation of God – Hebrews 1:1-4. It has always been interesting to me that when Moses asks God to show him his glory (Exodus 33:18) God promises that all his *goodness* will pass before Moses. However, Moses will not be allowed to see God's face, only his back. In II Corinthians 4:6, Paul asserts that in the *face* of Jesus God's glory is revealed. My thesis: if you want to begin to understand God's ways in the world, look *first* at the ministry and message of Jesus (including, of course, his death and resurrection). What was Jesus' attitude toward sickness, suffering, and death? Did he ever give any glib answers as to why people were suffering (blind, lame, etc.)? Do you find a message in Jesus' tears at the grave of Lazarus?

> *God answered Job from the wild whirlwind; Jesus answers us from the impotence of the cross. Put the question of your agony, doubt, bewilderment to Jesus. But don't go for your answer to Jesus quietly preaching the Sermon on the Mount. Don't go to Jesus riding triumphantly on Palm Sunday. Go only to Jesus hanging on the cross. He can answer you only from there.*[48]

---

47 Kreeft, Peter, *Making Sense Out of Suffering*, 112.
48 O'Malley, William J., *God: The Oldest Question*, 194.

A final word must be offered because the Gospel stories do not end with the crucifixion and burial. When everyone (including his followers) has written "finished" across the life and ministry of Jesus, God simply makes it a pause. The final word God speaks in Jesus is "resurrection." This is God's final answer to all the questions that swirl around the sufferings and tragedies of life.

My favorite chapter for funeral services is 1 Corinthians 15. You need to read it in its entirety for the total impact but I give you some excerpts with which to conclude a chapter which means to provide better questions to ask with the one place to look:

> *If there is no resurrection of the dead, then not even Christ has been raised. And if Christ has not been raised, our preaching is useless and so is your faith.*

> *If only for this life we have hope in Christ, we are to be pitied more than all others. But Christ has indeed been raised from the dead, the firstfruits of those who have fallen asleep.*

> *The last enemy to be destroyed is death.*

> *Therefore, my dear brothers and sisters, stand firm. Let nothing move you. Always give yourselves fully to the work of the Lord, because you know that your labor in the Lord is not in vain.*

Easter is God's answer to the questions that won't go away.

QUESTIONS FOR REFLECTION AND DISCUSSION

1. When and where are the times in your life when you feel you have learned the most?
2. Does it make any difference for you when the world is viewed as the vale of soul-making?

3. In the context of this chapter, do you think it helps to keep Romans 8:28 in mind: *We know that in everything God cooperates with us for good?*

4. Have you ever heard a sermon on Hebrews 5:8? How would you interpret such a text in the light of this chapter?

5. How does it make a difference on your concept of God to shift from the "back" of God's glory to the "front" of God's glory in the face of Jesus Christ?

25 STRATEGIES FOR LIVING IN A WORLD WHERE BAD THINGS HAPPEN

The word translated "repent" is perhaps one of the most misunderstood words in the New Testament. Too often it is interpreted as a command to feel sorrow and deep regret over transgressions and, if possible, accompanied by tears. The Greek word is much broader than that. It carries the meaning of a change of heart, a change of direction, a change of mind – a new way to see things. Both John the Baptizer and Jesus begin their ministries with "*Repent – the Kingdom (Reign) of God is at hand.*" True repentance has to do with having a "Kingdom mind" and seeing life with "Kingdom vision." It involves an entirely new attitude about life, faith, and the difficulties that come our way. It has to do with the basic philosophy we adopt as we seek to be Followers of the Way.

Psalm 118:24 provides the context for the strategies you will find listed below: *This is the day that the Lord has made; let us rejoice and be glad in it* (NRSV). The context includes not just that single verse but the chapter in which it stands. Psalm 118 begins and ends with identical verses: *Give thanks to the Lord, for he is good; his love endures forever.* This verse (118:1 and 118:29) together with verse 24 make excellent verses for establishing our mindsets at the beginning of each day.

In Mark 12:10-11 Jesus quotes Psalm 118:23 and applies it to himself: *The stone the builders rejected has become the cornerstone; the Lord has done this and it is marvelous in our eyes.* This probably originally referred to God's deliverance in the Exodus but was also applied to other acts of deliverance as well. That is what made the *day* one that the Lord had made (or the day on which he acted.)

Our new mindset begins with God's goodness and his faithful covenantal love established in Jesus Christ. (*"This is my blood of the covenant which is poured out for many."* – Mark 14:24). The new mindset of rejoicing begins with verse 23; God has inaugurated his new reign (Kingdom) in Jesus Christ but it has not yet come to its complete fulfillment. (That fulfillment is described in the book of Revelation.) But we believe that God is at work in his world and his commitment to us means we can trust him in the midst of whatever life throws at us.

As with most strategies for dealing with extremely difficult and long- standing problems, they are employed partially, haltingly, and in varying degrees of effectiveness. All require discipline, encouragement from others, prayer, and a large measure of Divine assistance. Patience with oneself is always necessary because some days will make it seem that no progress has been made. And, if you are like me, no point will be reached when you can say, "Well, I've finally dealt with that!"

All of the strategies come under the heading of "acceptance" in the most important course that life offers: Reality 101.

STRATEGIES: THINGS TO REMEMBER AND SOME THINGS TO DO, WHEN LIVING IN A WORLD WHERE BAD THINGS HAPPEN:

1. Life isn't fair.
2. Good and bad things happen to all people.
3. There is usually not a reasonable explanation as to why something bad happens.
4. There is no way to "bribe" God in order to be exempt from the chances and changes in life.
5. People do not need lectures or explanations when tragedy strikes – they basically need our presence.
6. We will not always feel God's presence when we need him most.
7. Questions and doubts are as much a part of faith as convictions and assurances.

8. God will cooperate with us for some good out of even the most tragic situations – if we permit him to do so.

9. Every tragedy comes with the question: "What can I do to lessen the hurt, grief, and pain in this situation?"

10. Life is a pilgrimage and we are on a journey.

11. The final resolution of all things will come only when there is a new heaven and a new earth.

12. The final rewards for righteous and holy living are promised in the next life.

13. Often, in this world, the first remain first and the last remain last.

14. However we describe it, evil is a reality in this world.

15. Staying in touch with our emotions and expressing our real feelings is necessary.

16. Most difficult questions are not easily answered and some questions are never answered.

17. We have a limited perspective – we can only see so much and we can only see so far.

18. We all need the ability to go on living creative and productive lives in spite of unanswered questions.

19. Instead of taking things for granted, we need to develop appreciation and gratitude for the simple blessings of everyday existence.

20. Every day we must find something to celebrate, regardless of how small or insignificant it might at first seem to be.

21. We all need a person, or persons, with whom we have established enough trust to be able to share our deepest hurts, our troubling questions, and our doubts and fears.

22. Assuming the role of victim doesn't pay any healthy dividends.

23. It is important to keep the accent on what we can do, where we are and as we are, with what we have.

24. As with the psalmists, when all is said and done, we try to keep our focus on God's everlasting covenant love.

25. In the midst of all our questions about God's lack of intervention, we must keep asking ourselves not "How is Jesus

like God?" but "What do we see clearly of God in the ministry, life, crucifixion, and resurrection of Jesus?"

Bibliography of Quoted Sources

Becker, Ernest. *The Denial of Death.* New York: The Free Press, 1973.

Claypool, John. *Tracks of a Fellow Struggler.* Waco: Word Books, 1974.

Dawn, Marva J. *Being Well When We're Ill.* Minneapolis: Augsburg Books, 2008.

Douglass, Frederick. *Narrative of the Life of Frederick Douglass.* New York: Fall River Press, 2012.

Fox, Michael J. *A Funny Thing Happened on the Way to the Future.* New York: Hyperion, 2010.

Frankl, Victor. *Man's Search for Meaning.* Boston: Beacon Press, 1959.

Gawnade, Atul. *Being Mortal.* New York: Metropolitan Books, 2014.

Geisler, Norman L. *If God, Why Evil?* Minneapolis: Bethany House, 2011.

Herman, Doug. *What Good Is God?* Grand Rapids: Baker Books, 2002.

Hick, John. *Evil and the God of Love.* New York: Harper & row, 1977.

Holloway, Richard. *Paradoxes of Christian Faith and Life.* Oxford: Mowbray, 1984.

Kreeft, Peter. *Making Sense Out of Suffering.* Ann Arbor: Servant Books, 1986.

Kushner, Harold S. Kushner. *When Bad Things Happen to Good People.* New York: Shocken Books, 1981.

Morris, Jonathan. *The Way to Serenity.* New York: HarperCollins, 2014.

O'Malley, William J. *God: The Oldest Question.* Chicago: Loyola Press, 2000.

Rees, Lawrence. *A New History.* New York: MJF books, 2005.

Sanford, John A. *The Shadow Side of Reality.* New York: Crossroad, 1984.

Washington Post, The.

Weatherhead, Leslie D. *Why Do Men Suffer?* New York: Abingdon-Cokesbury Press, 1936.

Wicks, Robert. *No Problem.* Notre Dame: Sorin Books, 2014.

Yancey, Philip. *Disappointment With God.* Grand Rapids: Zondervan Publishing House, 1988.

_____, *Where Is God When It Hurts?* Grand Rapids: Zondervan, 1990.

ALSO FROM ENERGION PUBLICATIONS

Finding God in Suffering is a wise, honest, and liberating approach to one of the most difficult questions we face.

Patricia Adams Farmer
Author of *Embracing a Beautiful God*

ALSO BY RON HIGDON

Every page of this book provides fresh insights gleaned from a long life of reading, thinking, and writing.

– John Lepper
Coordinator, Retired,
Cooperative Baptist Fellowship,
Kentucky

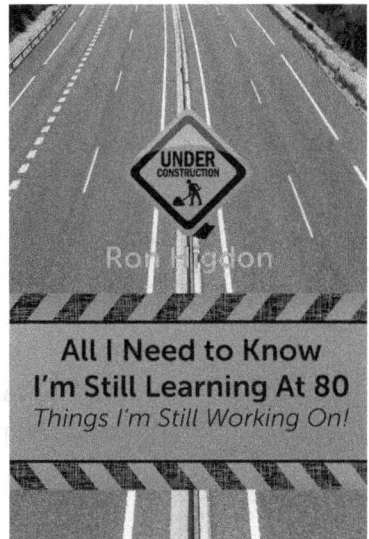

MORE FROM ENERGION PUBLICATIONS

Personal Study

Holy Smoke! Unholy Fire	Bob McKibben	$14.99
The Jesus Paradigm	David Alan Black	$17.99
When People Speak for God	Henry Neufeld	$17.99
The Sacred Journey	Chris Surber	$11.99

Christian Living

Faith in the Public Square	Robert D. Cornwall	$16.99
Grief: Finding the Candle of Light	Jody Neufeld	$8.99
Crossing the Street	Robert LaRochelle	$16.99
Life in the Spirit	J. Hamilton Weston	$12.99

Bible Study

Learning and Living Scripture	Lentz/Neufeld	$12.99
Inspiration: Hard Questions, Honest Answers	Alden Thompson	$29.99
Colossians & Philemon	Allan R. Bevere	$12.99
Ephesians: A Participatory Study Guide	Robert D. Cornwall	$9.99

Theology

Christian Archy	David Alan Black	$9.99
The Politics of Witness	Allan R. Bevere	$9.99
Ultimate Allegiance	Robert D. Cornwall	$9.99
From Here to Eternity	Bruce Epperly	$5.99
The Journey to the Undiscovered Country	William Powell Tuck	$9.99
Eschatology: A Participatory Study Guide	Edward W. H. Vick	$9.99
The Adventist's Dilemma	Edward W. H. Vick	$14.99

Ministry

Clergy Table Talk	Kent Ira Groff	$9.99
Thrive	Ruth Fletcher	$14.99
Out of the Office: A Theology of Ministry	Bob Cornwall	$9.99

Generous Quantity Discounts Available

Dealer Inquiries Welcome

Energion Publications — P.O. Box 841

Gonzalez, FL_ 32560

Website: http://energionpubs.com

Phone: (850) 525-3916

www.ingramcontent.com/pod-product-compliance
Lightning Source LLC
Chambersburg PA
CBHW031610040426
42452CB00006B/464